T0199187

COME DOWN, LITTLE BEAR

Story by Joanne Hyunjoo Lee

Pictures by Elizabeth Suh

The Bear

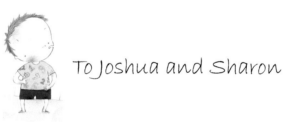

To Joshua and Sharon

COME DOWN, LITTLE BEAR

Story by Joanne Hyunjoo Lee   Pictures by Elizabeth Suh

Once there lived Little Bear.
One day the bear went out to
see what he could see.

The bear went over the mountain
to see what he could see.

**But the fountain dusty and dry
was all that he could see.**

The bear went down the road
to see what he could see.

But the toad sleepy and board
was all that he could see.

The bear went up the hill
to see what he could see.

But the windmill rusty and old
was all that he could see.

The bear went into the forest
to see what he could see.

But the guests dirty and messy
were all that he could see.

The bear went along the river
to see what he could see.

But the beavers busy with logs
were all that he could see.

The bear went to park
to see what he could see.

But the larks noisy with crumbs
were all that he could see.

The bear went into the cave
to see what he could see.

But Dear Dave who's never brave
was all that he could see.

The bear went up the tree
to see what he could see.

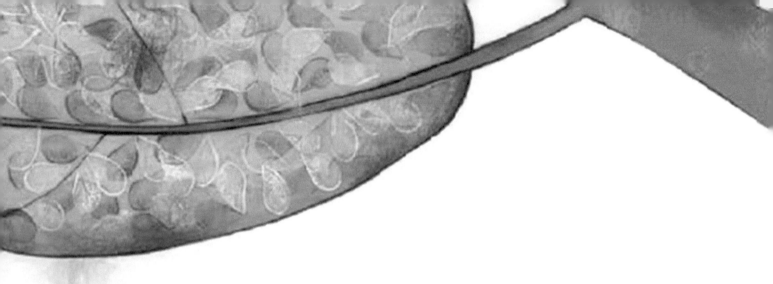

Then Mr. Crown who came to town said...

Come down, Little Bear.
I'm going to your house today.

So the bear welcomed him

with ALL HIS HEART!

Come down, Zacchaeus!
I'm going to your house today.
Luke 19:5

WestBow Press books may be ordered through booksellers or by contacting:

WestBow Press
A Division of Thomas Nelson & Zondervan
1663 Liberty Drive
Bloomington, IN 47403
www.westbowpress.com
844-714-3454

Interior Image Credit: Elizabeth Suh

ISBN: 978-1-6642-3067-5 (sc)
ISBN: 978-1-6642-3069-9 (hc)
ISBN: 978-1-6642-3068-2 (e)

Library of Congress Control Number: 2021907575

Print information available on the last page.

WestBow Press rev. date: 04/29/2021

WESTBOW
P R E S S®
A DIVISION OF THOMAS NELSON
& ZONDERVAN

Printed in the United States
by Baker & Taylor Publisher Services